Light, Float, Sit, Watsu ~ Virtually

Bodymind Electricity Sings to Me at Harbin Hot Springs & Other Traveling Poems

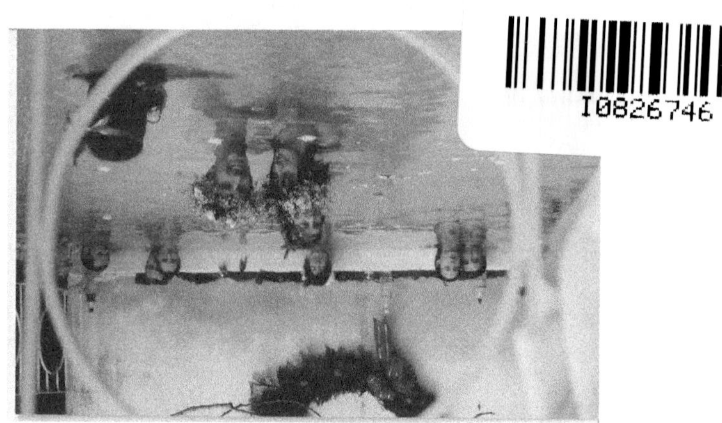

Scott GK MacLeod

Light, Float, Sit, Watsu ~ Virtually!

Bodymind electricity sings to me, o thee, who are pair, at Harbin Hot Springs

Scott MacLeod

Poetry Press at World University and School
San Francisco and Berkeley

Published by Poetry Press at World University and School
PO Box 442, Canyon, California 94516
info@worlduniversityandschool.org

Library of Congress Cataloguing-in-Publication Data
MacLeod III, Scott Gordon Kenneth, 1960-
Light, Float, Sit, Watsu ~ Virtually!: Bodymind electricity sings to me, o thee, who are pair, at Harbin Hot Springs / Scott MacLeod. p.cm.
Includes bibliographical references and index.
ISBN: 978-0-578-83468-9 1. Poetry. 2. I. Title.

British Library Cataloging-in-Publication Data is available

This book has been composed in Garamond

http://worlduniversityandschool.org/AcademicPress.html

Printed in the United States of America

10 9 8 7 6 5 4 3 2

CONTENTS

PREFACE

These poems in "Light, Float, Sit, Watsu ~ Virtually: Bodymind Electricity Sings to Me at Harbin Hot Springs & Other Traveling Poems," many written at Harbin or on the road to or from it, travel the globe from the Harbin warm pool, with a focus on meditation, to Cuttyhunk Island ('I kissed your back' & 'The bell was sailing off Canapitsit'), to India, and back to Santa Cruz, California. Most were written in 2012 and 2013.

I'd like to dedicate these poems to Sunheart, however, a friend and a main anthropological informant in my first book, "Naked Harbin Ethnography: Hippies, Warm Pools, Counterculture, Clothing-Optionality & Virtual Harbin" (2016) who passed away this autumn 2020. In the poem "She Dappled Sun" here, I seek to bring Sunheart a birthday torte, place one on his doorstep in the Harbin village, only to find out later that he's traveling far, far away. I'd like also to bring him alive again - with artificial intelligence and machine learning into avatar bot form - so that we might interact conversationally again, at first; see this December 18, 2020 UC Berkeley Anthropology Tourism Studies' talk in these regards - https://scott-macleod.blogspot.com/2020/12/doubledays-hummingbird-cynanthus.html - for both video and slides. I'd like to articulate Sunheart's Harbin knowledge and memories in digital form, and interactively, so that you or I might again talk and interact with him, as a first example of what might be possible in these regards (http://scott-macleod.blogspot.com/2020/12/gorse-sunheart-heartsong-at-harbin-hot.html?m=0).

Inherent in this Harbin poetry project, as well as in my actual-virtual Harbin Hot Springs' ethnographic project, with its poetry, is creating a realistic virtual Harbin with realistic avatar bots.

Scott MacLeod
New Year's Day 2021

Light, Float, Sit

Light
lights
Harbin
harmony
in one, waters warm,
immense, immersion, milieu *d'eau.*

Float
flies
in warm
watery
ease-me-in present,
a gift of flight in fluid *d'eau*,
where freedom finds releasing in among hug nude friends.

Sit,
roots
around,
touch all cells,
water pool food
intimate naked yes exchange,
of mind body suit seamlessly freeing we who connect under stars, skies,
Harbin-wise.

http://scott-macleod.blogspot.com/2013/09/swimming-iguana-email-to-cynefin-and.html

Bodymind electricity sings to me, o thee, who are pair

Bodymind electricity

sings to me, o thee,

who are pair,

and we,

sweet pear,

who sing harmony
in this spring.

Light in Napa

sparkles green and golden

on this fair day,

as I move on

toward Harbin.

Shimmering, shining

wondrous light,

how further to charge

this bodymind,

suffusing all-in with,

with love,

while traveling

through these tunnels of trees,

and on, along these winding roads?

Further travel,

and opening eyes,

with music sing-playing, -

but without you, as yet.

On, on, more

with love

underway,

on this fair day.

Omega-3, free,

neurophysiology,

and then ye, thee,

we, outstanding ~

see, musically, ...

and music happens.

Friends, of a jamming kind.

In the warm pool,

this vision vessel,

nudity frees,

and they cuddle~puddle,

dance Watsu Contact Improv,

breasts, bottoms,

bodymind shapes,

skin and curves,

beautiful people,

one man and three women

with nice bosoms,

happy, naturally, nature-ally,

erotically, and serene,

otter-like, -

haven't seen this in a while, -

play,

and I sit,

relaxation-'sponse-wise, ~

and, aware, find a kind of

unfolding, freeing oneness.

O, warm waters,

and beauties of Harbin.

The mind, the bodymind, as 3-D

holographic, imaging machine, ...

how to turn it on, welcome it, electricity-alive,

with a cello bow stroke,

with loving bliss,

in all these myriad qualities?

Turn on the Grateful Dead, Mozart, Ravi Shankar, J.S. Bach, -

you choose your music -

listen on your headphones,

yes, and find some such qualities

again, and again, a gain,

repeatedly, when you want …

but there are so, so many more bliss ~ qualities to explore.

How and when?

How to explore the new, freeing ones?

Why? ... because loving bliss-electric neurophysiologies

are some of the best experiences in life, and

can be both so awesomely intense,

as well as wondrously content.

What are these musical scores,

and music-improvisational themes,

for to start riffing …

Music unfolding ... for 5 decades ahead?

In the Harbin sauna,

after soaking free,

I went naked to dry and warm, -

for the night was cool, -

and therein I found six, nude people,

nearly full, and mostly women.

One couple - attractive, she particularly,

for me,

with long, dark hair, -

snuggled up close together,

with her man,

as if one,

content, her nipples half-visible,

touching her arms.

He was sitting kind of centered,

and she was inward, next to,

and kind of around him, and with.

This pair, a sweet pear,

seemed positively connected,

generating their own together-electricity,

almost as one, woman and man.

O' wonders of a naked, beautiful pairbond,

sitting skin to skin, having merged,

not sexually,

but partner-wise, in sauna,

on the lower bench,

near the heat.

Harbin is its own thing,

generating its own life, milieu,

and electricity, ~

from of the waters, out of the '60s,

out of the nudity -

and life flows here, with all its peculiarities,

the stuff of a tribe,

of residents, visitors and guests -

where the waters flow out of the ground,

in abundance,

and people come again and again,

to soak.

http://scott-macleod.blogspot.com/2012/04/bodymind-electricity-sings-to-me-o-thee.html

Illuminated Star Cloud: The dance or the pools? First the dance then the pools

The dance or the pools?

First the dance then the pools.
Long haired folks with
flowing clothes - wild and free.
What a shift -
from the city.

Listen first,
hear the rhythm,
dance a little,
cool, - then away.
Up to the pools,
past the Temple
with its white and
colored lights.

(A woman at the dance
is topless.
She starts to make out with
her friend on the pillows).
How glorious.

And Harbin's evening
illumination is all around.
So soft, - and
so nice to be back ...
Rainbow Gathering? ...
The moon is out,
the garden grasses
are high, and
the air is
fragrant.

I walk up and
there inside

Stonefront lodge,
I see her feet,
for she is lying
on her back
on a sofa, reading.

Past the Gazebo,
under the starlight,
I walk farther
up the way
past Redwood lodge
under the sun deck, and
into the pool area.
Welcome home.
It's dark.

I go into a bathroom,
shut the door,
and write some more -
this here now.

To the warm pool now,
leaving my clothes
on the benches
under the grape arbor.
To the pools.
In,
in ease under,
holding my ears,
float ...
Then to the shelf at one end,
and into lotus pose,
now relaxation response, MMmmm.

Inside, I go deeper -
she's pretty -
then out of the warmth
and into the hot pool.

In the dark,
the candle -
in its holder with holes
that illuminate
a heart image in metal -
looks like a golden brooch
on the neck of the
woman's bust
with flowers in her hair
above the whale spout.

The hot pool is
so beautiful
illuminated by candles
in many ways,
and steam,
in the night,
rises.

And there a woman
sits on
the dolphin railing stairs,
receiving the heat
of this earth's energy.

Out of the pool,
I head to shower,
skipping the
cold plunge,
and walk through
the dark pool area,
cement under foot -
it's joy to be walking
naked here -
to the new little deck
at the far end
of the pool area.
No one is around -

Stars -
then back,
put on my clothes
walk down through
Harbin again,
into the garden,
and past the temple

and to bed.

http://scott-macleod.blogspot.com/2010/05/illuminated-star-cloud-dance-or-pools.html - May 19, 2010)

In the space between warm water molecules, home at Harbin

In the space between,
warm water molecules,
home at Harbin

Fluid, water suit
fits all, in all ways,
connectingly.

Warm pool symbiosis,
unfolds fluently,
this water is live.

Encompassed in warmth,
releasing inside,
warm pool surrounds,
now.

Tao is,
in Harbin's warm water,
one-now.

Naked women are pretty,
Harbin pool area-wise, ~
biology.

People become
water birds,
bathing at Harbin.

One with nature,
Harbin's waters' warmth serene,
come again & again.

People wax water primates,
nature-returning,
warm pool nude oneness.

January sunshine,
people walk naked
in watery light.

Harbin's hippies
un-commune communally,
warm pool-wise.

No hippies here,
in Harbin's warmth ~
just naked, h2o be-ins.

https://scott-macleod.blogspot.com/2012/01/in-space-between-among-warm-water.html

Would like to sail

I'd like to sail
into loving bliss
like yachting
from one Greek isle to the next
nest, -
free, sun-open,
lovemaking much along the way,
via neurophysiologies of MDMA
ecstasy, -
of so many varieties and qualities
of our brain-chemistries, -
body-minded,
neural flowerings.

how?

Get onto the Greek craft,
with friends,
take the MDA,
then later explore
with music, with love between,
with generative creativity in singing words,
via connectings ...

Nature alive, free, compassionate
and wondrous, -
and for decades.

A progressive's dreaming
of innovating with human-being ...
happened tons in the '60s.

Let's explore that
sociocultural,
countercultural

way
toward these loves,
unfoldingly here now anew.

Musical scores
for this ...

and on computers ...

Chorus:

help the world
financially,
educationally,
help the poor.

https://scott-macleod.blogspot.com/2012/06/would-like-to-sail.html

I kissed your back

I kissed your back
as you lay naked on the sands
of Canapitsit, at tea time,
in early summer.

The half dome of the moon,
right side up in full day,
whitely illuminated,
by contrast, the blue sky around,
right over Gay Head,
240,000 miles away.

And you welcomed my soft kisses,
in the warm sun,
turning you on
ever so slightly,
and you moved just a little -
because doing so felt so good.

I wasn't sure as we lingered low
on the strand,
if I could see the highland, brown,
long haired cows,
on Nashawena,
across the channel,
but I thought I did see one.

Your beautiful hair
moved slightly in the breeze,
as my kisses journeyed
toward your bare neck,
and you received these,
nestling with the impulse, -
and almost rolled side-wards, -

but instead lingered
on your bare bosom, -
for who might wander by,
or come upon us, unexpectedly? ...
And this is Cuttyhunk
in modernity.

As a lad and a lass,
we might have adventured
here now into oneness,
together, heavenward, coitus,
but we wanted to explore
such over decades,
as musicians, as singers,
as contact improvisers,
as bliss-babies, and as lovers -

riffing together, bodymind-wise,
Grateful Dead-esque,
with unrolling jamming
of love-making, -

and so we dallied, without,
there on the beach,
my lips on your back.

Yet we were alive with
the receptivity of back kisses,
and moving, you rolled over,
for front kisses …
your nipples responding,
grace note and doubling-like, -
little musical embellishments,
bodymind-wise, -
and our music unfolded …

going into …

... don't think I'll finish this poem. :)

How would you? :)

http://scott-macleod.blogspot.com/2012/06/i-kissed-your-back.html

The bell was sailing off Canapitsit

The bell was sailing off Canapitsit,
as I cobbled by
on all those rounded stones.

Nashawena,
across the water passageway
of Canapitsit,
glistened green on
this summer day,
as I stood on Cuttyhunk
in wonder.

The waters flowed steadily southward
through it,
direction Martha's Vineyard,
in early summer
as I thought of her,
and the possibilities for joy
together.

These native names
rendered English by usage,
and from sail,
ring with a beauty of
this only somewhat
untouched-by-humans' landscape,
formerly forested,
which I now see one with, -
journeying through time,
(with much great sorrow, loss and passage), -
and shine in the now here,
by Canapitsit,
from Pocutahunconoh,

which is Cuttyhunk -
where also visited
Wampanoag peoples, I would guess,
and less likely speakers of
the Mi'kmaq language, -
and all Algonquins.
Native peoples, we remember
and envision
non-common-chimp-like history!

Were we together here singing,
holding hands, feeling softnesses,
of each others' arms,
beaming merrily together,
to riff with each other in joy, -
and with eyes, and smiles, especially, -
we might one here
in the lee
of this beach's bank,
to climax
in wonder and connecting, ~
and for kids?

But still - the sun shines -
and we have not yet
bodymind-joined, yet
may be connecting in thinking,
and with words,
as well as virtually, with our bodyminds,
while miles and miles away.
O Bonobos' love, ~
yet as unfolding duet.

Here by the waters of Canapitsit,
a red bell,
off in the distance,
sailed like a wind surfer,
as we began to sing,
and crescendo.
http://scott-macleod.blogspot.com/2012/07/bell-was-sailing-off-of-canapitsit.html

I started piping for

I started piping for
that little gaff-rigged yacht,
with brown foresail,
and a greenhouse for a cabin,
as it sailed into the pond
of Cuttyhunk,
past the Alert dock -

it was something about
its funkiness and freedom -
looking like a Chinese junk,
with a hippy woman
at its helm -
which inspired me to play.

Out, solo-sailing,
free and exploring,
I wanted to make music -
to bagpipe -
with its music
as it sailed in,
so I started to play,
and she smiled, and waved
from her craft,
holding her course
into this harbor
to anchor.

I had been playing just earlier,
awaiting the Alert ferry,
to pipe it in,
with old friends aboard.

The ferry came in,
the music happened, -
piping can soar, -
and in the melee of

people getting off,
communitas happens
on Cuttyhunk, at
ferry arrivals.

http://scott-macleod.blogspot.com/2012/07/i-started-piping-for.html

She dappled sun

She dappled sun
in grass green gold and oak
this illuminating afternoon
along the way,
in Lake County, California,
to Harbin.

Driving offered flying
Freedom
as I danced and rolled
with the curves on the road,
smooth-delighting in the
unfolding light
as music through
these tunnel trees
of forests, in sunbelt California -
dreamlike drive-movements of
slow-present-glide,
with blissing,
while descending the hill
from Mt. St. Helena
to Middletown.
Harbin
Valley offered slow,
and warm wet
and then ease
with oneness,
In the field, -
And I yielded
in this freedom …
soon in the flickering
blue waters.

But first I walked
to the half village,
near the Warehouse,

along its less trod path,
to bring Heartsong
a birthday torte,
raspberry, made in France
and procured in Napa,
a surprise on his doorstep
for the morrow.

Alighting to write
this,
along this way,
I smelled fragrance
in nature,
mint-ish, but suffusing the air,
and saw grapeleaves on
vines spread in around light,
rising also from the forest floor.

How to honor Heartsong's birthday
in specialness, and with care,
quietly, at Harbin,
for to generate loving energy
for him on this day?

I left at his door the torte,
as well as some little, neon, birthday candles,
only to find out later,
near the cold plunge and sauna,
that Heartsong is traveling,
far, far away, ~ and for weeks.

Heartsong offered torte
on his birthday
from his doormat
on a dappling sun,
illuminating day, -
thank you, and
happy birthday, Heartsong.

http://scott-macleod.blogspot.com/2012/09/she-dappled-sun.html

Watsu

In warm pool
chez Harbin,
both naked,

he turned her bodymind,
freely, in so many,
almost trippy, ways,

with skill, confidence,
and wonderful, therapeutic
assurance ~ normality in

meditative freedom,
in human wine cask rolling ...
an emergent, Harbin skill ...

and what lovely wine,
dancing together
in these wondrous waters!

http://scott-macleod.blogspot.com/2012/12/water-lily-flowers-in-warm-pool-chez.html

Monsieur Nikhil Bannerjee, master raga player, moved me along the way

Monsieur Nikhil Bannerjee,
master raga player,
moved me along the way,
on the road to Harbin,
sur la voie de Harbin.

'Afternoon Ragas:
Live in Amsterdam,'
became evening
soaking in the warm pool, -
space-making through
geothermal journeying,
with music,
avec de la musique.

Cloud-rainbow-beacon ~
light formation ~
in northern sky,
in kaleidoscopic, glorious,
afternoon Napa,
beamed steadily on
as I drove toward
the valley of Harbin,
dans la vallée de Harbin.

Bliss alive,
kiss of music-light-travel,
in natural world,
to beehive of healing …
at Harbin,
dear Harbin,
cher Harbin.

Can we do this online,
virtually, without mobility, -

or moving
in bodymind -
in our bathtubs, with
laptops, or
digital glasses, or
head bands, or
brainwave headsets, that
allow us to weave
narratives or music or visions,
together, in virtual worlds, or
via holography?
There are
generative possibilities
of creativity
ahead, via
interactive, movie realism …
and the relaxation response -
meditation in warm water,
méditation dans l'eau chaude …

as I,
poor wanderer,
move on,
from writing
by the side of the road,
toward Harbin,
riding sound waves
of musical light,
de la lumière musicale.

http://scott-macleod.blogspot.com/2013/01/yellow-corolla-monsieur-nikhil.html

The Gazebo Light Show at Harbin

I looked up
from down one flight of steps,
from in front of the restaurant doors,
and saw the shimmery, white
under-roof of the Harbin Gazebo
Dance-reflecting its fountain's movements
on that rainy night.

Went to bed,
with rain on my head …

As I walked in in the morn,
the long way around,
from across the creek,
near the Res Center,
on up the road
to the village path,
and then through the woods
to the pools,
for to see things and to hike,
it was three turkeys,
on the bubbling, creek side of the road,
one male,
with white head and red underface,
and a little blue in there too -
so colorful, vivid, clear and bright,
thanks to nature on this moist morning -
that inspired me to write this,
catalyzed by the
Magnificent, shimmery light
of the Gazebo under-roof
on a rainy night,
which I had never seen before,
at light-filled Harbin.

As I walked on,
I stepped into
one of Harbin's nice, new
bathrooms for campers,
and for the people of
the (somewhat new) canvas-covered Domes,
popping up on Harbin hillsides, -
like little, puffball mushrooms, in the rain, -
near the Harbin, bubble Domes' junction,
to write,
since smartphone use
at Harbin isn't allowed,
except in parking lots,
to which this bathroom is near.

These new restrooms are beauts:
3, orange-globe, light fixtures,
suggestive of apples in shape,
and a decorative, ceramic, sink basin, -
blue, green and flowery,
with a little orange here in there, too, -
and shimmery, silver, upper walls, in tile,
with one sun - a rise or set - in orange tiles,
at the horizon, at midriff's height,
with blue tiles below
~~~ and spacious ~~~
with only a toilet, and no shower,
and six, blue, ceramic nobbies,
on the double-decker, 3-prong, coat rack,
an earthen-orange floor below,
and one rectangular skylight,
high above.

Walked on to the pools …

~~~ ~~~ ~~~

Disconnect and soak, and
tune into the lands and the waters.
Waters flow upward here,

and earth's energies too …
while things bubble around …
reconnecting with
what comes up,
in the oneness which is Harbin.

On into the waters
from O:) that night's Gazebo show …

O:), the light, the watery light.

http://scott-macleod.blogspot.com/2013/03/the-gazebo-light-show-at-harbin.html

Resplendent Quetzal: Light lumens illuminated lightly

Light lumens illuminated lightly

The way to the pools' warm,
At night, moon-wise,
At Harbin.

What lovely, pied moonlight,
dappling all around.

http://scott-macleod.blogspot.com/2013/11/resplendent-quetzal-light-lumens.html

Big, green, iridescent forests speak to me in Oregon, on the road to Reed

Big, green, iridescent forests
speak to me in Oregon, ~
and blue skies and gray clouds
color everything,
with wild, different light.

Timbering industry lumbers on,
as Old Growth forests diminish,
as I drive north to Stumptown,
not yet in a solar car,
to Reed's ReedFayre,
a reunion in Portland,
which is growing big
with people.

Reed's canyon -
that green water-valley in its middle, full of life,
this campus's natural focus these days, -
old friends,
a gentler, Oregon ethos,
than many, in modernity,
are welcomingly familiar,
and I speak quietly here to folks
of World University and School,
influenced as it is,
in its knowledge generation focus, especially,
by Reed's
intellectual culture.

I wander down
on a tour,
into the depths of its library,
to the calligraphic Lloyd Reynolds' collection,
and learn of a book,

full of Beat poets and writing-art,
"LJR: Stained the Water Clear a Festschrift for Lloyd J Reynolds,"
a long time Reed professor,
whom didn't teach Steve Jobs calligraphy -
that was Father Palladino -
before Jobs dropped out,
turned on,
moved back to the Bay,
to found Apple with Woz,
in a garage.
A Lloyd Reynolds' weathergram,
10 words or less calligraphed, about nature,
on paper,
preferably cut from an old, brown bag,
dangles from a tree,
like a treat,
outside the library,
which didn't say,

'Big, green, iridescent forests
speak to me, on the road to Oregon,'

but instead was writ with, ~

"The new buds open from within,
are lit from behind"

http://scott-macleod.blogspot.com/2013/06/big-green-iridescent-forests-speak-to.html

Sounds in the night in Kolkata (Calcutta), India, Tagore's "A Moments Indulgence", I lie in my bed in the home of the parents

Sounds in the night
in Kolkata (Calcutta), India
are many and varied ...

Car horns' combined
at 4 in the morning
sound like a dinosaurs' gathering, ...

Clink, clink, clink - the metal pole
hits the ground, ...
the night watchman sounds
like he's awake around 2, 3 and 4 ...

This city is vibrant and awake
in the dream night ...

first Muslim call to prayer at 5 am
in this predominantly Hindu city
where Bengali and Hindi and English
are much spoken ...

a sound system turns on ...

someone starts singing ...

a group of women walk by talking ...

is that a snare drum? ...

and all so early in this sound-alive morning.

And the recent Sikh parade
was so colorful, and celebratory,
with garlands festooning the trucks ..

Religious parades are still many here,
and almost kind of hippy ...

We visited Tagore's house yesterday ...

*

Here's Tagore ~

'A Moments Indulgence

I ask for a moment's indulgence to sit by thy side. The works
that I have in hand I will finish afterwards.

Away from the sight of thy face my heart knows no rest nor respite,
and my work becomes an endless toil in a shoreless sea of toil.

Today the summer has come at my window with its sighs and
murmurs; and
the bees are plying their minstrelsy at the court of the flowering grove.

Now it is time to sit quite, face to face with thee, and to sing
dedication of life in this silent and overflowing leisure.'

Rabindranath Tagore

*

I lie in my bed
in the home of the parents,
my friends,
of my best friend from high school,

listening to sounds in the night,
in Kolkata (Calcutta),
in west Bengal,
here in India! ...
and, lingering,
wonder about
sitting, quite, with you,
and singing the
music of bliss loving, ~
a kind of Krishna consciousness,
having visited Mayapur first today ~
face to face,
bodymind with bodymind,
and especially with love and care.

http://scott-macleod.blogspot.com/2013/12/eastern-great-egret-sounds-in-night-in.html

Elephant seals: Santa Cruz, on New Year's Day

Santa Cruz, on New Year's Day

People on the street,
with backpacks
and long hair,
colorful clothes,
a little down & out, -
that western, freedom thing, -
and sunny, comfortable weather,
I'm heading for
Dance Church of Santa Cruz, ~
first time ever.

The trip is fast
from the S.F. Bay,
on Sunday morning,
on a Spare the Air Day,
per the radio,
to this still alternative city.

The winding road,
17 South,
begins, and
the world changes
into Santa Cruz,
northern California.

Getting to the dance late,
exploring a little,
I may head to see the
elephant seals
at Año Nuevo,
later today.
It's breeding season.

The front door
is getting locked,
and the man wearing a Fez, says
'Want in?'
And I say 'Is this Dance Church?'
'Yea, it's just over,' he says.
'Can I just see the space?' I ask.
'Yea,' he says,
'but another class is just coming in.'
I walk in the front door
of 418 Front Street,
passing among the dancers, -
all relaxed, chatting, happy,
alternative types,
in colorful, loose clothing, -
and out the main, side door.
I may try to camp
the night before,
and come
another time.

I walk into downtown Santa Cruz,
from Front, along Cathcart Street,
to Pacific Ave., with all its businesses, -
Latino ones, especially.
There are a lot of
alternative types here, too.
The revolution is happening,
in a low-key way,
and, from the 1960s,
both business- ,
and California-wise,
in this beach city.
I imagine business practices
in Santa Cruz are humane,
and compassionate,
and people-friendly, -
yet with still a lot of
street people on-the-ground.
The weather is great today.

I hear
nice guitar, with slide,
by that old long-hair,
sitting on a bench on Pacific Ave.,
on such a beautiful, sunny day.

I walk
down to the Town Clock,
which looks like a bell tower,
at the end of Pacific, -
it seems like the nicest part
of this avenue,
but few people are here.
Sunday motorcyclists
roll in, dressed in black,
two by two,
revving their engines, -
on a New Year's ride.

I head into the
great bookstore,
Bookshop Santa Cruz,
and am transported,
into the world of words,
and exploration.
O, the relaxation response, ~
with books!

I head on, exploring,
via the Quaker Meeting House,
which I've never visited before,
with a large peace sign
under its eaves,
toward Año Nuevo.
Stopping at Whale City Bakery,
north of Santa Cruz, -
it's crowded, ...
"Crazy," the waitress says
about this.

The warmth in the air
feels like Global Warming.
Will this coastline
diminish 20 feet in my life time,
as the oceans rise?

Año Nuevo,
with its breeding,
elephant seals,
costs $10 to park,
and all the tours,
with rangers,
are booked for the day,
so I continue northward,
detouring to
Pigeon Point Light House,
with its Youth Hostel,
with hot tub.
A lot of people are visiting today.

A frowsy group of motorcyclists,
their black leather all asunder,
are waddling back to their hogs,
from their tourist stop;
don't know if they're the same
folks as above.
First time it hasn't rained
in eight years
on New Year's Day,
per the cashier in the gift shop,
(who enjoys the Half Moon Bay sailing club
with Cal 20s and Lasers :)
some motorcyclists told her, earlier.

I walk in toward the coast,
past the Youth Hostel.
A great docent,
in the hall
with the restored, Fresnel light,
a radiant jewel -

picture all those lenses,
beaming beehive-like
in your mind -
is giving a talk.
With a slight, English accent,
and possibly the training of an actor,
he engages his listeners,
as raconteur,
talking of this gem
of a beacon light,
to help with ocean navigation.

Back to Canyon,
and a call from
a dear, old friend ...

a birthday exploration,
the day after,
in beautiful California ...
yea to travel ... :)

https://scott-macleod.blogspot.com/2012/01/elephant-seals-santa-cruz-on-new-years.html

Harbin Waters' Cosmic Consciousness

One fig leaf dropped,
golden in the warm pool,
right in front of me – plop.

Meditating in lotus pose
in warm water I was, and then
drops another golden, fig leaf,
to my right, but a little browner,

from green~golden fig trees above.
Easing inwardly myself near the stairs,
she who is naked beautiful walks in,

with lovely face, bosom, and hair,
finding ease, in the warmth.
She looks at me – connection.

In the hot pool, next door,
finding heated~water, immersive openings,
she comes in, once standing in

water near her long-haired, male friend.
Are they connected?
She is beautiful in so many ways,

proportional, nude, serene in being,
connectable – but with friend, probably,
a traveling companion, it seems.

Back in the warm pool,
I emerge heading for the hot pool again,
and get a little dizzy, biologically,

and, aware, observe how this
could be similar to a biological or
chemical door of perception opening

to Cosmic Consciousness,
in another context.
But what is the code

to open these doors, neurophysiologically –
and for all kinds of brain and bodymind

freedoms and transformations,

naturally, but made real
with entheogens and
Mozart and Raga and the Grateful Dead

as well as India, Hindu and Harbin cultures?
How to open the doors,
warm pools-wise,

to eliciting loving bliss, and
to cosmic consciousness?

Further pool play welcome.

http://scott-macleod.blogspot.com/2013/10/blue-bird-of-paradise-harbin-waters.html

NOTES ON THE POEMS

In these 'Light, Float, Sit, Watsu ~Virtually,' Harbin and traveling poems, Watsu refers to water shiatsu, a kind of water dance, and therapeutic modality, significantly developed at Harbin.

Bodymind is a word I use in these poems to join the often dualistic separation, linguistically, of the words body and mind, and also to refocus connotations of consciousness with regards to the mind-body problem, and in relation to Heart Consciousness Church, aka Harbin Hot Springs. The word *oneness* in these poems has been significant at Harbin over the years in these regards as well. See, for example, Harbin's current founder Ishvara's book "Oneness In Living: Kundalini Yoga, the Spiritual Path, and the Intentional Community" as well as this pamphlet "Heart Consciousness Church - 1975-2015 - 40 Years of Living the Future - Harbin Hot Springs" - http://www.harbin.org/wp-content/uploads/2015/01/Harbin_40th_anniversary.pdf.

In the poem "Monsieur Nikhil Bannerjee, master raga player, moved me along the way," and with regards to science and studying consciousness, too, – Raga is the improvisational form of classical Indian music, where in the north of India, students begin their study of ragas by learning to sing raga compositions (called bandish).

In "Light, Float, Sit, Watsu ~Virtually! … " I've added a blog link with every poem, where in these blog posts, you will also find photographs.

Names of poems with natural images in beginning of title are sometimes related to the poem, and sometimes arbitrary.

The cover photo is "The Marriage in the Harbin warm pool – 2001," the same photo from the cover of my large book "Naked Harbin Ethnography: Hippies, Warm Pools, Counterculture, Clothing-Optionality and Virtual Harbin" (thanks, Stormy!), - now turned upside down.

Thanks again to the startup Poetry Press at World University & School, which has once again kindly published my book.
http://worlduniversityandschool.org/AcademicPress.html
http://scottmacleod.com/

Scott MacLeod - https://twitter.com/scottmacleod
World Univ and Sch Twitter - http://twitter.com/WorldUnivandSch
Languages - World Univ - http://twitter.com/sgkmacleod
WUaS Press - https://twitter.com/WUaSPress
"Naked Harbin Ethnography" book (in Academic Press at WUaS) - http://twitter.com/HarbinBook
OpenBand (Berkeley) - https://twitter.com/TheOpenBand

ABOUT THE AUTHOR

Scott MacLeod is a professor of anthropology, founder and president of the virtual wiki World University and School. He is the author of the books "Naked Harbin Ethnography: Hippies, Warm Pools, Counterculture, Clothing-Optionality and Virtual Harbin" (2016), "Haiku~ish and Other, Loving, Hippy, Harbin Poetry" (2017), "Winding Road Rainbow: Harbin, Wandering & the Poetry of Loving Bliss" (2018), "To the Dance or the Pools? ~ Virtually! How different it is to soak at Harbin Hot Springs, than to realize it in virtual Reality" (2019), Scott MacLeods' "Honey in the Bag" Scottish Small Pipes' bagpiping album (2020), and "Light, Float, Sit, Watsu ~ Virtually: Bodymind Electricity Sings to Me at Harbin Hot Springs & Other Traveling Poems" (2021).

Scott MacLeod, author (credit: Scott MacLeod)

Jacket design: Scott MacLeod
Cover photo: Scott MacLeod
Author photo: Scott MacLeod

Scott MacLeod's poetry and anthropology books are all published in the Press at World University and School, a new publishing house, and accessible from - https://www.amazon.com/author/scottmacleodworlduniversity - and the musical album is published by Scott MacLeod's Arts, accessible here - https://scottmacleodhoneyinthebagscottishsmallpipesbagpiping.bandcamp.com/ - and - http://scottmacleod.com/piping.htm.

Academic Press at World University and School
ISBN: 978-0-578-83468-9 (Press at World University and School)

FIN

www.ingramcontent.com/pod-product-compliance
Lightning Source LLC
LaVergne TN
LVHW050610100826
845148LV00015B/3211

* 9 7 8 0 5 7 8 8 3 4 6 8 9 *